Boys and Girls

written by
Deborah Williams

KAEDEN BOOKS™

Table of Contents

Singing 4
Basketball 6
Reading. 8
Soccer 10
Dancing 12
Baseball 14
Ice Skating 16
Glossary 19
Index. 20

Singing

What do boys and girls like to do?
Girls like to sing.

Boys do too.

Basketball

Boys like to play **basketball**.

hoop or basket

basketball

basketball court

Girls do too.

Reading

Girls like to read.

Boys do too.

Soccer

Soccer is the most popular sport in the world.

Boys like to play **soccer**.

shin guards

soccer cleats

Girls do too.

Dancing

Ballet shoes are also called ballet slippers.

Girls like to dance.

Boys do too.

Baseball

Boys like to play **baseball**.

glove

Girls do too.

Ice Skating

ice rink

Girls like to ice skate.

Hockey players wear a lot of safety equipment because it is a high-contact sport.

Boys do too.

17

Boys and girls like doing the same kinds of things.

Glossary

baseball – a game between two teams in which players try to score runs by hitting a ball with a bat and running around the bases

basketball – a game between two teams in which players try to score points by shooting the ball into the basket

soccer – a game between two teams in which players try to score goals by kicking the ball into the net

Index

baseball 14

basketball 6, 7

boys 4, 5, 6, 9, 10, 13, 14, 17, 18

dance 12

girls 4, 7, 8, 11, 12, 15, 16, 18

ice skate 16

read 8

sing 4

soccer 10, 11